I0797281

Words that are tricky to understand are in **bold**. Find out what they mean in the glossary.

Words that are difficult to say are in *italics*. Find out how to say them at the back of the book.

WHAT IS PETROLOGY?

Petrology is the scientific study of rocks, including the **minerals** they're made of, their **composition**, and how they were formed and affect the planet. It is a branch of **geology**.

The scientists who study petrology are called **PETROLOGISTS.**

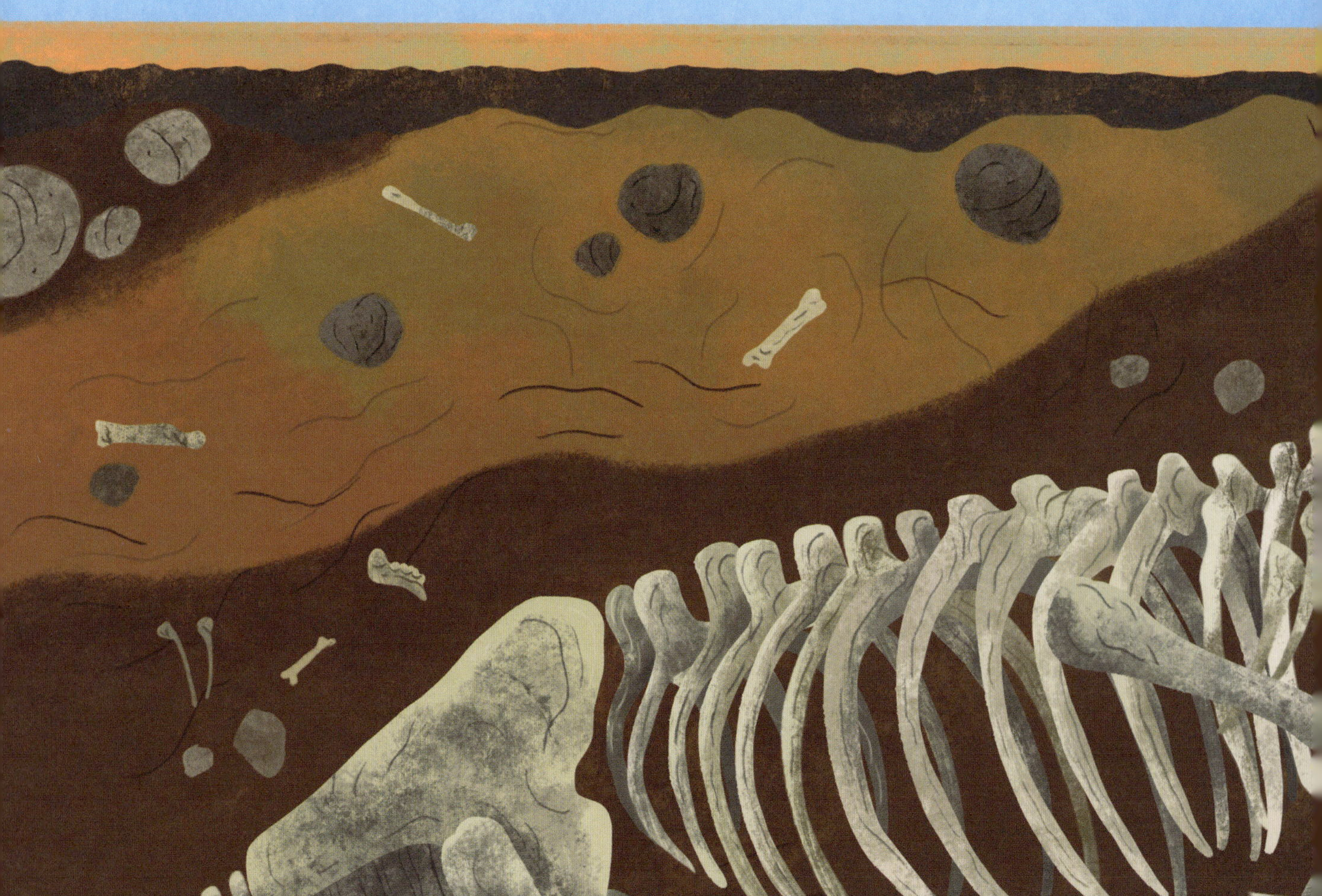

DO ROCKS SHAPE THE EARTH?

DISCOVER THE SCIENCE BEHIND **PETROLOGY**

(pet-ROH-luh-jee)

Written by Olivia Watson

Illustrated by Daniel Limon

Some people think rocks are small and dull, but the world is full of incredible rocky landscapes – from towering cliffs and columns, to twisting waves and caves.

Everything on Earth is connected to rocks because the planet's surface – called the crust – is made of rock! No matter their shape, size, or location, rocks all have a story to tell – one shaped by time, **pressure**, temperature, and lots of surprises.

Petrologists know Earth has always been a rocky planet, even though it hasn't always looked like it does today. Over 4 billion years ago, Earth was a fiery world covered in **molten** rock! It had no oceans and no life – just scorching heat and swirling **lava**.

Then it cooled, forming a rocky crust. But the crust didn't stay still, it kept moving, shifting, and changing shape...

In fact, Earth's surface is always moving! The crust is made of huge slabs of rock called tectonic plates which all land and oceans sit on. These plates have the strength to

move entire continents!

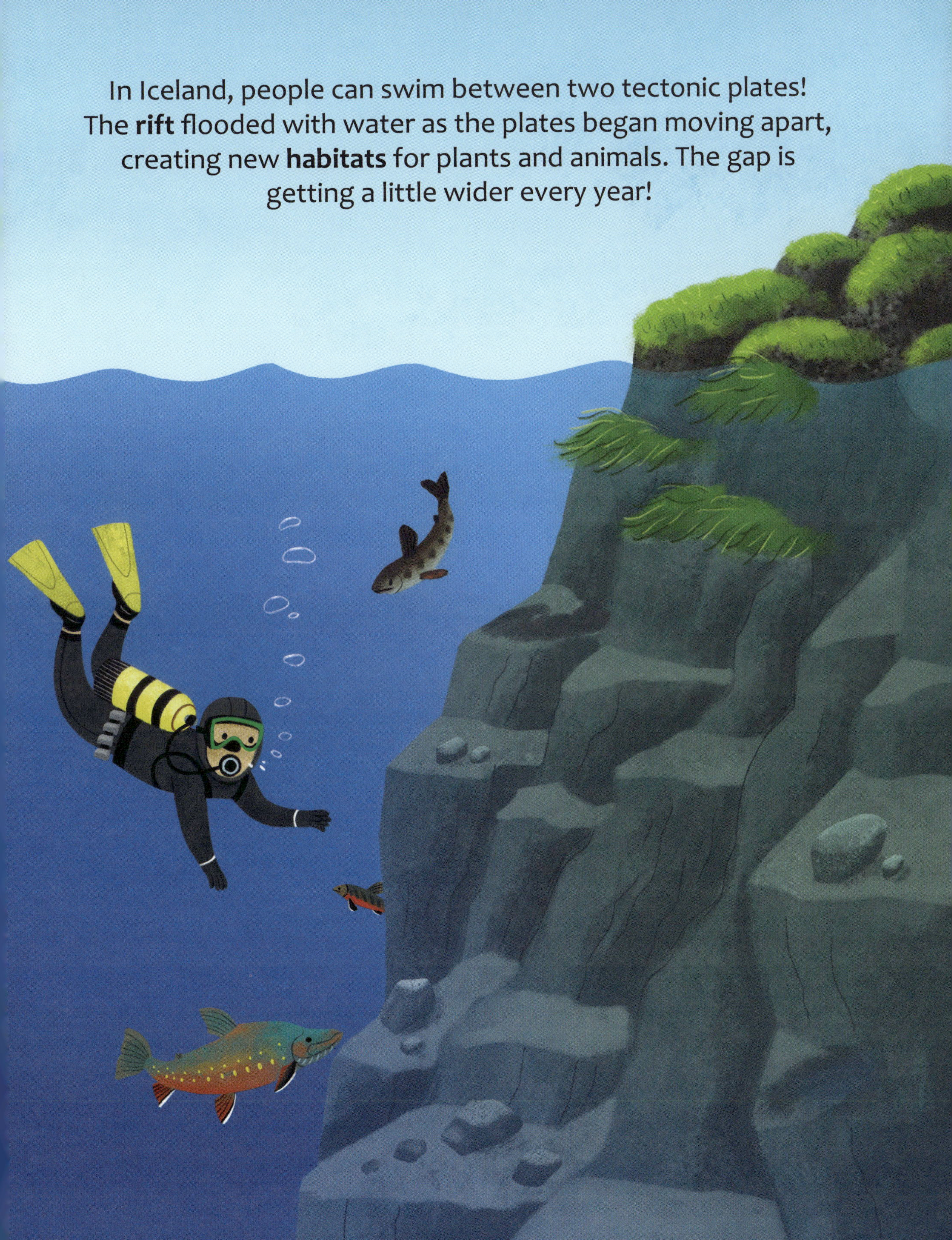

In Iceland, people can swim between two tectonic plates! The **rift** flooded with water as the plates began moving apart, creating new **habitats** for plants and animals. The gap is getting a little wider every year!

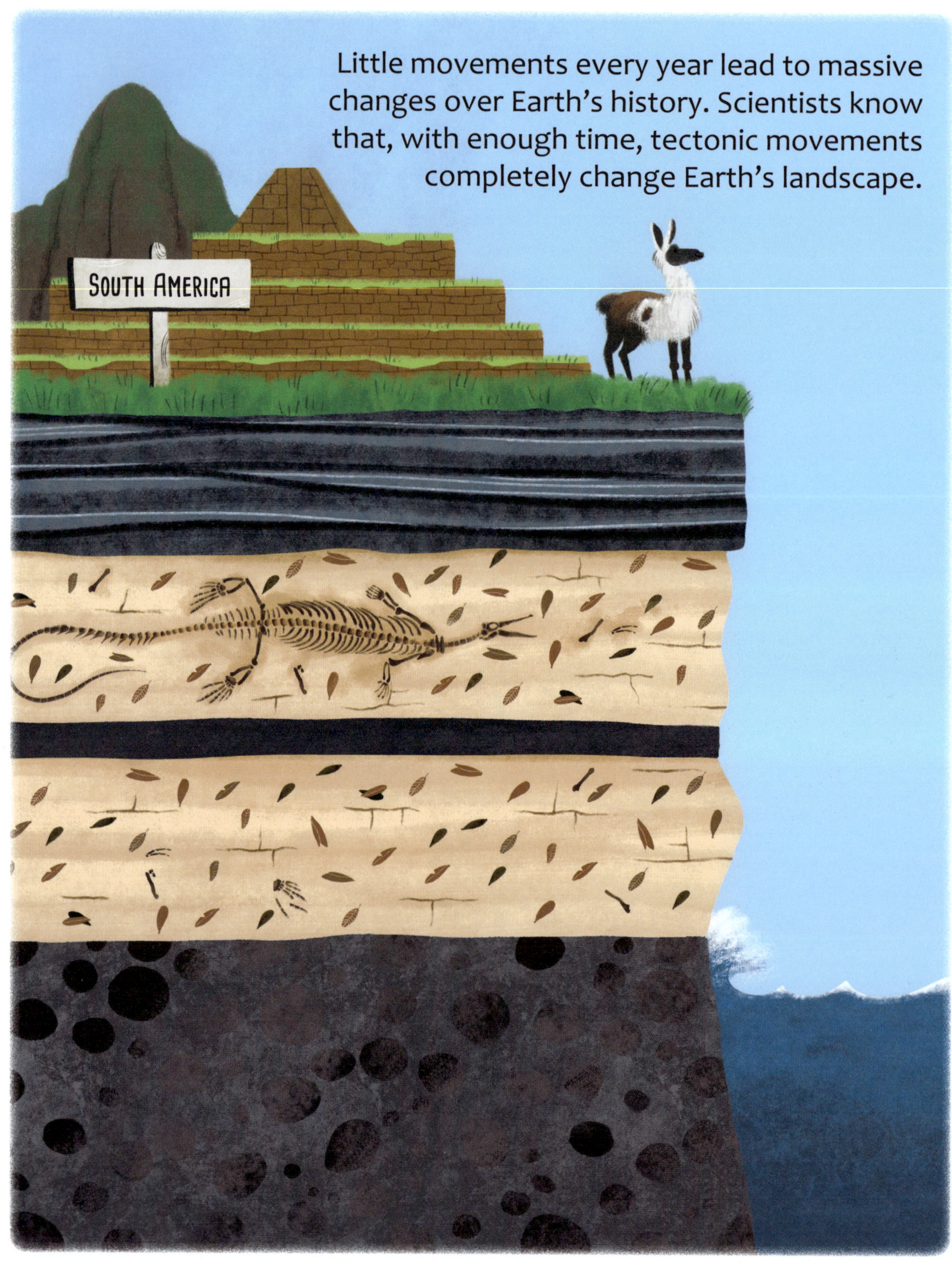

Little movements every year lead to massive changes over Earth's history. Scientists know that, with enough time, tectonic movements completely change Earth's landscape.

Petrologists have found identical layers of rocks and **fossils** on **coastlines** on opposite sides of an ocean. This shows that, millions of years ago, the **continents** were joined together as one huge piece of land!

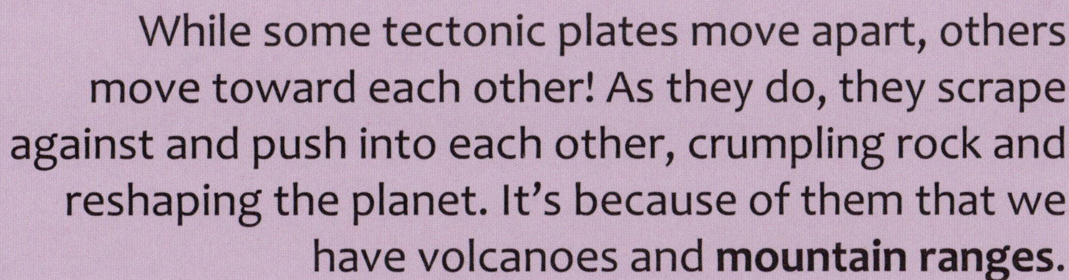

While some tectonic plates move apart, others move toward each other! As they do, they scrape against and push into each other, crumpling rock and reshaping the planet. It's because of them that we have volcanoes and **mountain ranges**.

But even mountains are constantly changing – scientists have discovered that Mount Everest is **getting taller every year!**

Petrologists don't just look at how rocks affect Earth's landscapes, they also look at how Earth's landscapes affect rocks. Over time, wind and water wear away soft rock, carving incredible shapes.

Some rock structures, like the Twelve Apostles in Australia, have turned into famous natural landmarks.

But impressive rock structures don't just rise into the sky, they can form under Earth's surface too.

Underground caves are important habitats for many animals. Bats, blind fish, and creepy crawlies all live in these cold, dark homes where **stalactites** and **stalagmites** form rocky obstacle courses.

Huge rock formations make a big difference to the natural world, but so do small rocks! As rocks become worn by wind and water, they break into tiny grains called sediment or sand.

This means the materials they're made of can flow into the soil around them, like *phosphorus* and *potassium* which make soil healthier and better for plants to grow.

Learning what rocks are made of is one of a petrologist's most important jobs. By slicing up rocks and studying them under a **microscope**, petrologists can see all the amazing minerals inside. Zoomed in, their collection of crystals look just like a **beautiful kaleidoscope!**

BASALT

SCHIST

GABBRO

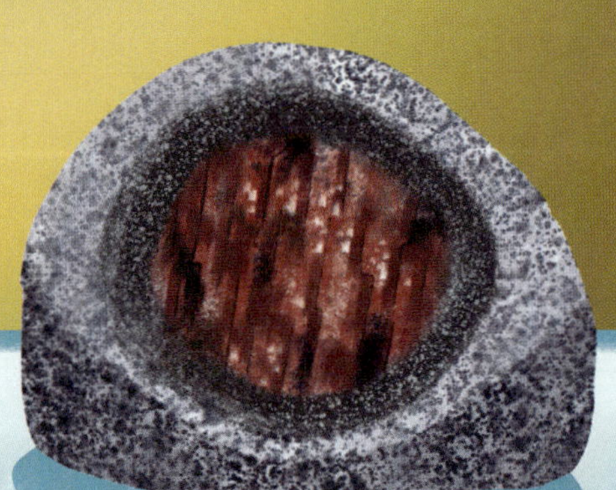

GARNET AMPHIBOLITE

LIMESTONE

MARBLE

Minerals affect how rocks look on the inside and outside, but their appearance isn't set in stone. Intense heat from volcanoes or pressure underground can completely transform rocks...

resizing their minerals, allowing new minerals to grow, and giving them different **properties**. Thanks to Earth's powerful influence, rocks are changing all the time, like

natural shape-shifters!

Rocks can be made of amazing minerals. Many people **mine** them for metals like nickel and iron which are used to make batteries and cars, tin and copper which are used to make electronics, and **precious** gemstones.

Rocks are also an incredibly useful building material. They're strong and last a long time, which makes them perfect for building roads, bridges, and even castles!

As well as teaching us about the world around us, rocks and their minerals teach us about the past.

Sometimes, the remains of plants and animals get trapped in rock and stay hidden for millions of years. When scientists dig up fossils, they learn what life was like long ago, like when **dinosaurs ruled the Earth!**

Thanks to petrologists, we know that rocks shape Earth and will continue to do so for billions of years.

But importantly, we know that as well as shaping our surroundings, rocks influence our lives, our cultures, and our understanding of this special planet we call home.

Record-breaking

ROCKS

Rocks may shape the Earth, but that's not the only impressive thing about them. These rocks are all record breakers worth celebrating.

The lightest rock is... PUMICE!

Pumice is full of holes, which let air into the rock. This makes it so light that it can float on water!

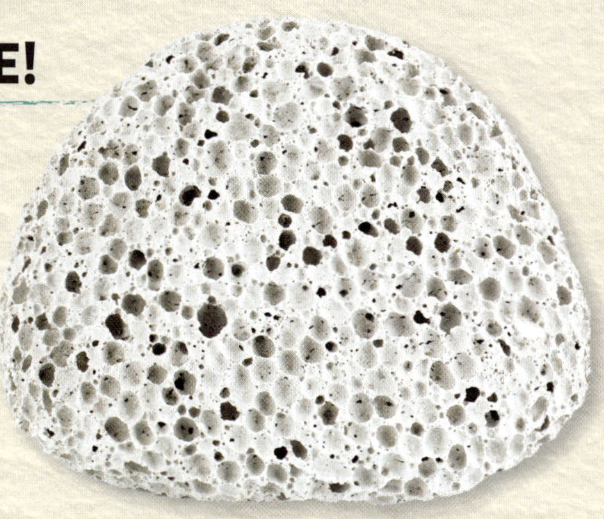

The heaviest rock is... PERIDOTITE!

Peridotite is made up of heavy minerals like olivine and metals like iron. It's this composition that makes peridotite so **dense**.

The most magnetic rock is... **LODESTONE!**

This rock naturally attracts metal, just like a magnet! Early explorers used it to make compasses, which helped them navigate through the wilderness.

The oldest rocks are... **BILLIONS OF YEARS OLD!**

Earth's oldest rocks are around 4 billion years old. But the oldest rock ever found seems to be a **meteorite** which contains grains that are 7 billion years old! It came from outer space before landing on Earth.

The biggest rock is... **MOUNT AUGUSTUS!**

Located in Australia, this rock is 2,350 feet (715 m) tall and almost 5 miles (8 km) long! It's called Burringurrah by the local people who consider it a very special place.

Groundbreaking

ROCK FACTS

There's so much to discover about the world of petrology. Did you know these fascinating facts about rocks?

ARE ROCKS ALWAYS DULL IN APPEARANCE?

No! Rocks can be stunning in shape and pattern. Some minerals even glow under certain conditions, making the rocks even more stunning.

HOW FAR DO ROCKS MOVE?

Incredible distances! Scientists have found fossils of ocean animals at the top of mountains, which shows that land that's high up today was once deep underwater.

WHAT OTHER WAYS DO WE USE ROCKS?

Rocks and their minerals are used everywhere! They're even used in toothpaste, paint, TVs, paper, and cat litter. We come into contact with rocks in surprising ways every day.

CAN PETROLOGY HELP WITH GLOBAL WARMING?

Yes! Scientists have found a way to turn **carbon dioxide** into rock. When in the air, this harmful gas speeds up **global warming**, so this smart technique could really help the planet.

IS EARTH THE ONLY ROCKY PLANET?

No! Lots of other planets are made of rock too, including Mars. It's often called the "Red Planet" because its rocks have so much rusty iron inside that they look red!

GLOSSARY

Carbon dioxide – an invisible gas in the air that plants take in to make food and oxygen.

Coastlines – areas where land meets the sea.

Composition – everything that makes up a material, including the amounts and structure of each thing.

Continents – the huge pieces of land on Earth. For example, Africa and North America are separate continents.

Dense – tightly compacted.

Fossils – the remains or impression of plants and animals that lived long ago.

Geology – the study of the physical planet Earth. It's studied by geologists. *Need help saying this? Look below!*

Global warming – the rising temperature of the planet over time.

Habitats – the places where animals and plants live.

Lava – hot, melted rock on Earth's surface.

Meteorite – a small piece of space rock that has fallen to Earth's surface.

Microscope – a scientific tool that makes small things look much bigger.

Mine – dig up.

Minerals – substances that are naturally found in things like rocks, sand, and soil.

Molten – melted.

Mountain ranges – a group of mountains that are close together, often in a line.

Precious – something that is special, rare, or that people care for.

Pressure – the force of something pressing down on, or against, something else.

Properties – the qualities or features something has, like its shape or how it feels.

Rift – a crack or gap that has opened in the ground.

Stalactites – formations that are made from minerals (see left), but look like icicles and grow down from cave ceilings.

Stalagmites – formations that are made from minerals (see left), but look like icicles and grow up from cave floors.

HOW DO I SAY?

Geologists
jee-OH-luh-jists

Geology
jee-OH-luh-jee

Gneiss
nee-s

Kaleidoscope
kah-LY-dah-scope

Petrologists
pet-ROH-luh-jists

Petrology
pet-ROH-luh-jee

Phosphorus
FOSS-fuh-russ

Potassium
puh-TAH-see-um

THE BIG QUESTIONS ANSWERED

This is more than just a series of books; it is a complete resource.
Accompanying each book is a variety of FREE material to engage curious kids with science.

www.thebigquestionsanswered.com

Use the QR code to visit the website, download free resources, and discover other books in the series.

On the website, find out incredible things about petrologists, including what they do, some of their greatest discoveries, and the people who have made a difference in this field of science.

The material is also available for home or classroom use, supporting all the information in this book.

Teachers' & Parents' Resources
With discussion prompts, questions, and extra information around key topics.

Activity Pack
Fun activities including creative writing, word searches, and more.

Audio Book
Experience this book in audio, narrated by a professional voice actor.

The Big Questions Answered is published by Beetle Books.
Beetle Books is an imprint of Hungry Tomato Ltd.

First published in 2026 by Hungry Tomato Ltd
F15, Old Bakery Studios, Blewetts Wharf, Malpas Road,
Truro, Cornwall, TR1 1QH, UK.

ISBN 9781835691533

Copyright © 2026 Hungry Tomato Ltd

No part of this publication may be reproduced, stored in a retrieval system, or transmitted in any form or by any means, electronic, mechanical, photocopying, recording, or otherwise, without prior written permission of the copyright owner.

A CIP catalog record for this book is available from the British Library.

With thanks to:
Editors: Holly Thornton and Jenny Rowan
Designers: Meg Holbrook and Amy Harvey
The team at Beehive Illustration
Consultant: Dr Hannah Hughes

Information in this book is up to date as of the time of writing.

Printed and bound in China.

Picture Credits:
(t = top, b = bottom, m = middle, l = left, r = right)
Shutterstock: Artsiom P 35bl; Chris Howey 35mr; Indralsmna22 34mr; Janelle Lugge 32-33b;KrimKate 32bl; Merlin74 34bl; Nmedia 35tl;Stas Malyarevsky 32mr; Vadim Sadovski 33mr.

Wikipedia: By Ryan Somma - [1], CC BY-SA 2.0, https://commons.wikimedia.org/w/index.php?curid=5228830 33tl.